George's Bright Idea

Ian Whybrow ✳ Vincent Vigla

OXFORD

UNIVERSITY PRESS

George was lazy. All day long, George played computer games. He only stopped playing computer games to watch TV. George let his mum and dad do all the work.

George's mum and dad had a little café called *Fresh Fish*. They worked hard but they didn't make much money.

One day, lazy George was watching TV. The phone rang. Lizzie, the childminder, didn't hear the phone. George ignored it. The ringing went on and on. Finally, George dragged the phone across the floor.

"Is that you, George?" said his dad.

"Yeah," said George.

"Please can you come and help at the café?" asked Dad. "It needs a good clean. Bring some rubber gloves with you."

"Me?" asked George.

"Yes you, George," said Dad.

George did not like being dragged away from the TV. He liked it even less when he had to help at the café. Worst of all, he would miss his favourite TV show, *Monster Trucks*.

George stomped into the kitchen and found the gloves.

He stomped outside to tell Lizzie that he was going to the café.

Then he stomped into the garage to get his bike.

7

At the café, there was only one customer.
But there were lots of pans to clean.
"Why can't you get a dishwasher?"
George grumbled.

Dad sighed. "We can't afford it, George. Business is bad. People like hamburgers better than fish."

George's mouth fell open. He didn't know things were *that* bad. So George didn't complain as much as usual. He helped to do the washing up.

When he had finished, George's mum kissed
his cheek.

"Take this fish pie home for your supper," she
said. "It's your favourite." She looked sad and tired.

George stomped up the front steps and slammed the door.

"I'm back!" he shouted to Lizzie. Lizzie didn't hear.

George put the fish pie into the microwave. Then he put it on a tray. He sat down in front of the TV. The fish pie was delicious.

"How could anyone like hamburgers better than this?" he called out loud. Lizzie didn't hear.

George wanted to change channels. But he couldn't find the TV zapper. He searched down the back of the sofa.

George found the TV zapper.

He also found ...

... some keys,

... Mum's ring,

... a toy

... and a magazine.

The room looked a mess. George remembered his mum's sad, tired face. He remembered his dad's gloomy voice. "I know! I'll clean up for them," he thought.

First he went to the kitchen to wash his plate. Lizzie looked worn out. So George said, "Come and watch TV while I clean up." He felt great when he finished.

Then George sat down. He started to read the magazine he had found. When his parents came home, they were amazed. George was reading and the room was clean. They saw all the things that George had found.

Eating fish is good for your brain

"My ring!" Mum laughed. "I thought I had lost it forever!"

"And there are my keys!" Dad said with a big grin.

Mum gave not-so-lazy George a hug. She said, "Thank you George. Business is bad but at least the house looks tidier!"

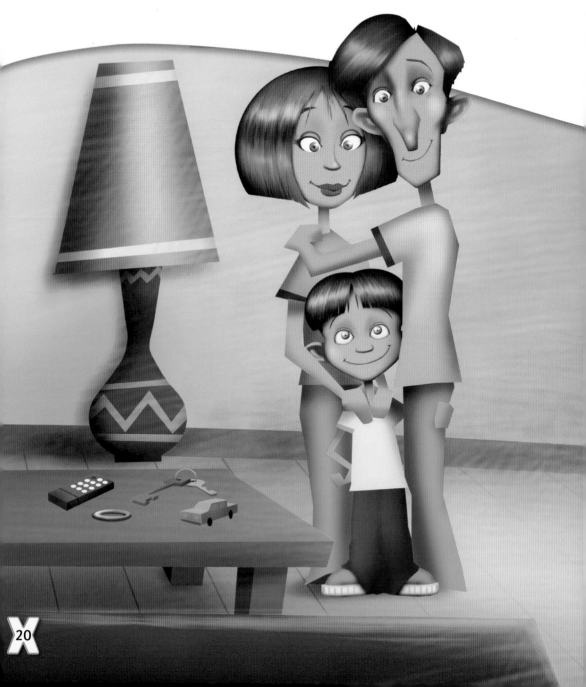

Then George thought about something he had read in the magazine. It said, "Eating fish is good for your brain!" That gave him a bright idea.

Eating fish is good for your brain

Three months later, George rode his bike to the café. It was full. He stopped and looked up. A bright new sign over the café said *Brain Food*. Dad came out.

"Want some help?" asked George.

"Yes please! We're really busy, thanks to you!" Dad said proudly. "Our new name has made all the difference. Where did you get a bright idea like that?"

"Down the back of the sofa," said George.

CAFÉ
CULTURE